COUNTRY WALKS IN MIRFIELD, EMLEY, THORNHILL AND DENBY DALE

17 circular walks

by
Douglas Cossar and John Lieberg

for The Ramblers' Association West Riding Area

Other publications by the Ramblers' Association (West Riding Area)

Dales Way Handbook (with the Dales Way Association, annually)
Kiddiwalks (new edition Spring 1995)
Douglas Cossar, *Ramblers' Leeds,* 2nd edition, Volume 1 East of Leeds (1999)
Douglas Cossar, *Ramblers' Leeds,* 2nd edition, Volume 2 West of Leeds (2000)
Douglas Cossar, *The Airedale Way* (1996)
Douglas Cossar, *Ramblers' Wakefield* (1997)
Marje Wilson, *The Brontë Way* (1997)
Douglas Cossar, *Ramblers' Bradford,* Volume 1 (1999)
Walks in and around Kirklees
More Walks in and around Kirklees

This new, enlarged edition of
Country Walks in Mirfield, Emley and Thornhill first published 2002

RAMBLERS' ASSOCIATION (WEST RIDING AREA)
27 Cookridge Avenue, Leeds LS16 7NA

ISBN 1 901184 30 7

Cover photographs
Front: Stile near Emley.
Back: Denby Dale Viaduct; on Thornhill Edge; Shepley Lock.

Publishers' Note
At the time of publication all footpaths used in these walks were designated as public rights of way or permissive footpaths, or were paths over which access has traditionally not been denied, but it should be borne in mind that diversion orders may be made or permissions removed. Although every care has been taken in the preparation of this guide, neither the author nor the publisher can accept responsibility for those who stray from the routes described.

Contents

The Country Code

Guard against all risk of fire.

Take your litter home.

Fasten all gates.

Help to keep all water clean.

Keep dogs under control.

Protect wild life, plants and trees.

Keep to public paths across farm land.

Take special care on country roads.

Use gates and stiles to cross fences, hedges and walls.

Make no unnecessary noise.

Leave livestock, crops and machinery alone.

Enjoy the countryside and respect its life and work.

The **Ramblers' Association**, a registered charity, is an organisation dedicated to the preservation and care of the countryside and its network of footpaths, and to helping people to appreciate and enjoy them.

Through its Central Office the Ramblers' Association lobbies and campaigns for more effective legislation to achieve

- the preservation and improvement of the footpath network
- better access to the countryside
- the preservation and enhancement for the benefit of the public of the beauty of the countryside.

Since its formation in 1935 the Ramblers' Association has grown into a powerful campaigning organisation with a membership of 132,000.

The Association relies on many volunteers working at Area and Local Group level to help achieve these objectives.

The **West Riding Area** is one of the 51 Areas of the Ramblers' Association which cover England, Wales and Scotland. It includes the whole of West Yorkshire and parts of North Yorkshire around Selby, York, Harrogate, Ripon, Skipton and Settle, as well as the southern part of the Yorkshire Dales National Park. The Area has over 4,000 members and is divided into 13 Local Groups.

The **Local Groups** carry out the work of the Ramblers' Association by keeping an eye on the state of footpaths in their area and monitoring proposed closures and diversions.

- They put pressure on their Local Authority to take action to remove obstructions and re-instate footpaths after ploughing.
- They do practical work of footpath clearance and waymarking, and can erect stiles and footbridges.
- Where the Local Authority has set up consultation procedures, e.g. Footpath Forums, the Local Group will normally send a representative.
- Many Local Groups produce their own programme of walks.

Regular walks are a very important part of Ramblers' activities. As well as ensuring that local footpaths are used, they provide healthy recreation and the opportunity to make new friends.

If you use and enjoy the footpath network, please help us to protect it, by joining the Ramblers' Association. For further information contact

The Ramblers' Association, 2nd Floor, Camelford House, 87-90 Albert Embankment, London SE1 7TW (Tel.: 020 7339 8500, Fax.: 020 7339 8501; e-mail: ramblers@london.ramblers.org.uk).

Or visit our website: www.ramblers.org.uk

Authors' note

In 1983 the Dewsbury and District Group of the Ramblers' Association published a booklet of eight walks called *Country Walks from Mirfield and Thornhill*. This proved so popular that in 1989 a second booklet appeared, covering a slightly larger area, called *Country Walks in Mirfield, Emley and Thornhill*. In time copyright of these two publications passed to the West Riding Area of the Ramblers' Association, who reprinted the second one, but both have now been out of print for several years.

Demand locally continues strong, so the decision was taken to produce a larger book of walks, covering again a larger area, which would use ideas from the two previous volumes but would be substantially a new publication.

The countryside between Mirfield and Denby Dale is a rewarding one for the walker. Being part of the South Pennines, it is hilly, which makes for variety and produces many fine views, although this can also make some walks more strenuous than their mere distance might suggest. It is criss-crossed by footpaths and tracks, many of considerable antiquity, as the frequent remains of causeying testify. Although mainly pastoral, arable fields are also encountered, and there is much woodland, at its best at bluebell time or in autumn. Stone-built villages and hamlets, old farmhouses and halls provide architectural interest, mills and canals will attract the industrial archaeologist.

Almost all the walks are within Kirklees Metropolitan District, although we do stray once or twice into Wakefield or Barnsley. They can all be located on the Ordnance Survey Landranger Sheets 110 Sheffield & Huddersfield and 104 Leeds & Bradford (at a scale of 1:50 000) or, of more use to walkers because the scale is 1:25 000, on Explorer 288 Bradford & Huddersfield, although Walk 14 does stray briefly onto Sheet 278 Sheffield & Barnsley. The sketch maps which accompany each walk are based on these Explorer maps and are reproduced with the permission of the Controller of H.M.S.O. They are intended to give an overview of the walk and to supplement the description, but as they are greatly simplified, particularly in built-up areas, **they should not be used as a substitute for the description**.

Please read the descriptions carefully: we have tried to make them clear and unambiguous and to eliminate the risk of misinterpretation. In our experience lots of walkers go astray through not concentrating on the text of a walk, inadvertently skipping a line or jumping by mistake from one stile to the next, or just losing the place through being engrossed in conversation with their companions!

All the paths used are definitive rights of way or permissive footpaths. At the time of writing one or two are obstructed by fallen trees, but these can be negotiated with care, and a number of stiles are in poor repair. If you should encounter any obstacles, obstructions, nuisances or other difficulties, please report them to the Rights of Way Officer, Kirklees Metropolitan District Council, Flint Street, Fartown, Huddersfield HD1 6LG (tel: 01484-225565). You should not encounter any hazards on the walks, but do look out for bulls at large in pastures in the summer months and take suitable evasive action, even if this means a minor trespass. Better safe than sorry!

You will encounter several waymarked long-distance paths in this area, particularly the Kirklees Way, for which a new guidebook is just about to be published, the Brontë Way (for which the Ramblers' Association also publishes a guide) and the Spen Valley Heritage Trail in the north and the Dearne Way and the Barnsley Boundary Walk in the south. The Emley Boundary Way is a 14-mile walk around Emley, for which a descriptive leaflet is available locally, as are leaflets for the Emley, Denby Dale, Skelmanthorpe and Clayton West Village Trails.

All the walks are accessible by public transport, and we have given details as they are known to us at the moment. But please do check this information with West Yorkshire Metro (Tel: 0113-245-7676).

Happy walking!

Douglas Cossar/John Lieberg
April 2002

WHERE DO THE WALKS START?

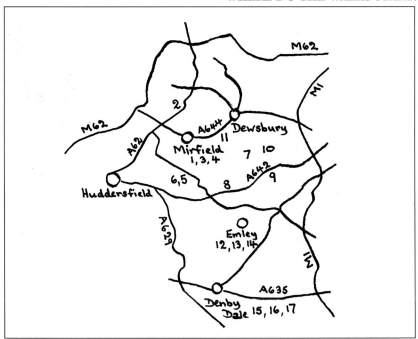

CROSSLEY, NORRISTHORPE AND NORTHORPE

WALK 1

5¼ miles (8½ km). Mirfield is rich in old ginnels. This walk uses a selection of them, along with tracks and field paths, to climb to Norristhorpe. There are some fine buildings on the way. Surprisingly rural.

By bus: There are buses from Huddersfield, Leeds, Dewsbury, Bradford and Wakefield to Mirfield. Get off at the Library and walk down Station Road, turning right at the canal bridge down onto the towpath.
By train: There are trains from Huddersfield, Dewsbury, Leeds and Wakefield to Mirfield on the Huddersfield line. Leave the station and walk up Station Road towards the centre of Mirfield, cross the canal and turn left down to the towpath.
By car: Park in Mirfield Library car park (pay & display), leave it and turn right down Station Road, turning right at the canal bridge down onto the towpath.

Follow the towpath past Mirfield Boat Yard and Ledgard Flood Lock, pass under a road and continue on the path by the River Calder. Soon the path turns sharp right between walls, then sharp left again. At the end of the ginnel bear right to the main road, cross it diagonally left and take the track opposite, which leads to another ginnel, which leads to

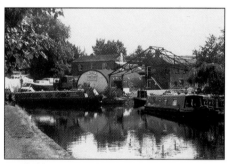

Mirfield Boat Yard

another road. Cross and turn left for a few yards, and at the end of the brick house take the paved path on the right, in a few yards ignoring other paved paths forking right off it. By one of several "No Cycling" notices fork left off the paved path up a tarmac path. On reaching a street turn right, but where the street curves sharp left, fork right off it along a paved path to the next road. Cross straight over into Knowl Park.

Walk up the left hand edge of the park, turn left with the fence and follow it to an exit and a short ginnel. Turn right up the street, and at the T-junction at the top cross and take the ginnel opposite. Look out for a fork, where you keep right, along a short tarmac ginnel to a street. Walk down the street, and at the T-junction cross straight over to take the tarmac ginnel opposite. At the end turn sharp left with playing fields to the right. On reaching a T-junction of paths, turn right, and soon the path turns sharp left again. When you reach a track, keep forward along it, but where it turns right, keep straight forward along a narrow enclosed path. Walk up a few broad steps and turn left, in a few yards ignoring further steps on the right, and follow the old paved path to the next road, bearing right as you reach it.

Cross the road, go up the steps and along the fenced path opposite, with a cricket ground to the left. Cross two streets and follow the path to a lane, cross diagonally right to the stile opposite and walk along the right hand edge of the field. Do not pass through the next stile, but at it turn sharp left - Balderstone Hall is half right - and continue along the right hand edge of the field. Walk through two fields and into an enclosed path with school playing fields over the hedge on the left. Keep straight on to a road (Crossley Lane) and turn left along it.

Ignoring all side-roads and public footpath signs, keep on along the road, but immediately after it turns sharp left at Hill Top Farm cross the stile on the right, drop to another stile, cross a track to another stile and walk straight down the right hand edge of the field to a stile at the bottom. Drop by steps to the beck, ford it by the stones or the tyres, and climb the steps up the other side. Cross a stile into a field and cross the field diagonally to a stile in the top right hand corner (you may find the going easier if you bear right and walk round the edge of the field). Bear right along the track and follow it through the farmyard at Owlet Hurst.

Where the track begins to climb, by a lamppost on the right, fork right along a path to a stile by a gate. The path continues by the hedge on the left, passes to the left of a wooden pylon and goes through a stile on the left. Follow the left hand edge of two fields to the road in Norristhorpe.

Northorpe Hall

8

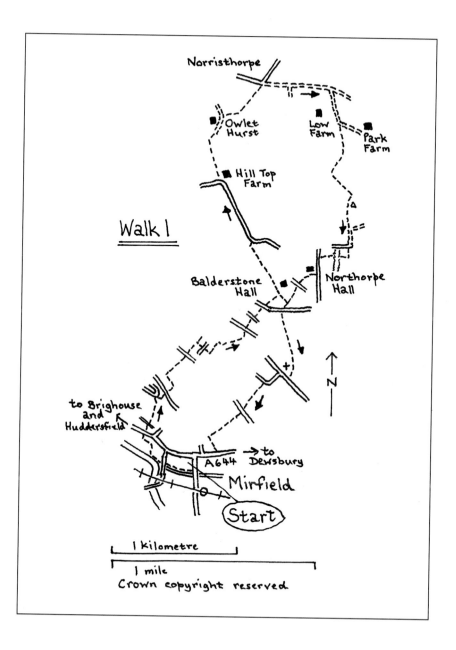

Norristhorpe

Owlet Hurst

Low Farm

Park Farm

Hill Top Farm

Walk 1

Balderstone Hall

Northorpe Hall

N

to Brighouse and Huddersfield

to Dewsbury

A644

Mirfield

Start

1 Kilometre

1 mile

Crown copyright reserved

9

Turn right and in a few yards, before the United Reformed Church, fork right along a broad track (Lodge Lane). Ignore a track on the right leading to Low Farm. Well before you reach Park Farm, take a green lane forking right, and when the enclosed section ends, keep straight on, down between hawthorns, with a fence on the right, to a stone bridge. Cross the right hand of the two stiles and walk up the left hand edge of the field to another stile. Cross it and turn left, to follow the fence/hedge on the left, turning right with it in the next corner. In the top corner of the field cross a stile on the left beside a gate, cross a former railway line and turn right over a stile by a gate along a track. *(Note an Ordnance Survey column a short way along on the left - the only one in Mirfield.)* You are joined by another track from the left.

On reaching a terrace of cottages, the track becomes tarmac (Jill Lane). Shortly after it starts to bend right, fork left off it over a stile by a gate and walk along the track. Where this ends, keep forward, passing a stile by a gate on the left; 5 yards further on turn sharp right across the field to a gap-stile at the foot of the railway embankment. Go through the tunnel under the railway, cross the stile and walk forward over the next field, picking up a wall on the left, to another stile, where you rejoin Jill Lane.

Turn left. The road climbs and then descends again. Follow the old paved path just to the right of it. Soon this bears right along the drive of the stately Northorpe Hall. Don't continue bearing right to the house, but follow the track to a signposted gap in the brick wall on the left; pass through and cross the grass to a ginnel which leads down some steps into Crossley Lane. Cross the lane to a stile to the right of a gate and bear half right up the field to pass about 20 yards to the left of a climbing frame, then keep the same direction over the next field to join Balderstone Hall Lane.

Turn left. At the next road turn right for 15 yards, then cross it and pass between bollards into a ginnel. Cross over a street and continue along the ginnel, which ends at a field. Go half right to a gap in the churchyard wall, pass through and turn left, soon crossing a cross path to reach a wall corner. Follow the paved path along with a

Mirfield stocks

wall on the right, and when the paving ends, keep on along the path to pass between the old tower and the 19th-century Mirfield Parish Church. *A blue plaque gives information about the history of the church.*

Go through the stile and bear right *(notice the stocks to the left)* past the main gate to the church, cross the road and go down Pinfold Lane opposite, using a pleasant path through the trees. At the foot ignore Vicarage Meadow on the left, 30 yards further on ignore a signposted footpath on the left, but 5 yards further on take another signposted footpath to the left of a red brick house, a ginnel between high walls. Follow it to the next road, cross and turn left for a few yards to find the next ginnel on the right. The path soon leads down the right hand edge of a large grassy area, at the end of which take the left fork down to the main road. Turn right to return to the centre of Mirfield.

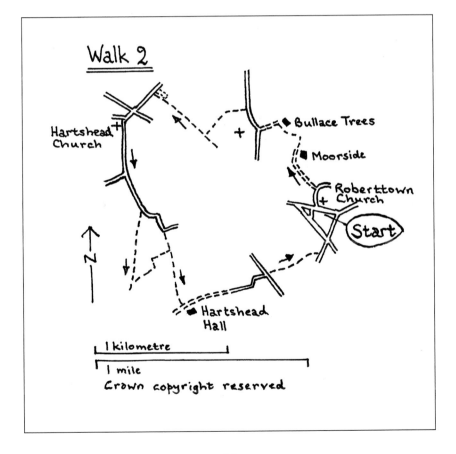

11

ROBERTTOWN AND HARTSHEAD

WALK 2

3¾ miles (6 km). A circular walk from Roberttown Church on field paths and old lanes, with panoramic views.

By bus: The 217/219/221 Huddersfield-Leeds (3 an hour weekdays, 2 an hour Sundays) 250/253/258 Wakefield-Bradford (2 an hour weekdays, Sundays hourly) pass through Roberttown.
By car: Street parking near Roberttown Church.

The walk starts down the lane to the left of Roberttown Church, and where the lane bends right, fork left off it along a track. Follow the track straight through the yard of Moorside Farm, passing to the left of the attractive brick house, and continue along a narrower path. Cross a stile by a gate ahead (ignore the stile on the right) after which the path bears left. At Bullace Trees Farm the path joins the farm access track, which you follow to the next road, reaching it at Triangle Farm. Cross to the footway and turn right to pass Liversedge Cemetery. About 100 yards further on go through the stile by a gate on the left and along the track, then follow the left hand edge of the field. Bear slightly left with the hedge and walk up the edge of a second field. At the top turn right along a cross path.

Follow the path to the next road. Just before you reach it there is a fenced area on the right. *This is a Quaker Burial Ground known as "The Sepulchre", where four members of the Greene family were buried in the late 17th century. The Greenes were a very well known family, firstly in Littletown as yeomen and later as clothiers in Hightown. It is unusual to see Quaker graves with such elaborate tombstones, which give detailed inscriptions about the Greenes.*

Turn left up the road, and at the crossroads carry straight on to Hartshead Church. *From 1811-15, during the time of the Luddite riots, the Revd Patrick Brontë was curate here. A corner of the churchyard is said to contain the unmarked graves of men who lost their lives in the riots. The earliest date found in the*

Hartshead Church

church is 1611 on one of the two sundials. There are signs of Saxon work at the base of the Norman tower, and two fine Norman arches. The church was restored in 1881, when the stained glass windows were fitted. There is the stump of an ancient yew tree in the churchyard, probably older than the church itself, and it is said that one of Robin Hood's bows was made from this tree.

Pass the church along the road, and enjoy fine views to Castle Hill and West Nab, and where the road bends right carry straight on downhill (Hartshead Lane) to pass the Gray Ox Inn. Keep on downhill and pass a house on the left, cross the road and find a signed footpath between two gateposts, labelled "Three Nuns". Go along this path, with a young plantation on both sides, for about 70 yards, then turn left along an old field boundary, soon with a hedge on the left. At the bottom of the field cross the bridge and walk in a straight line across the next two fields to a track junction.

The ancient yew tree

Turn left up the track (straight ahead leads to the Three Nuns). It bends left and leads to a stile, after which you are on a narrow enclosed footpath. Where the path widens out and there is a stone wall ahead, turn right over a stile and go steeply downhill with a hedge on the right. Cross a stile ahead into a path with a fence on the left, which you follow down to another stile. Keep forward to cross a footbridge, then continue down the right hand edge of the next field to cross a stone slab bridge. Walk uphill towards a copse of trees, where you reach a cross path. Turn left, go through a gate and keep forward along the tarmac lane.

For a time you lose the tarmac surface, but it re-starts and you pass some attractive houses. Carry on to the next road. Cross the road and pass through the stone stile and walk up the field on the line of the trees ahead. You will pass a footpath sign in the middle of the field, where you bear slightly left to pass to the left of a metal pylon and reach a stile in the top left hand corner of the field. Look back as you climb for the last panoramic view of the walk. Turn left up the road, and just before the Star Inn turn left along Commonside, and ignoring access roads to houses on the right, where a tarmac road forks off to the right, follow it to the next road and turn right to the church.

BY BOYFE HALL TO UPPER HOPTON AND DRANSFIELD HILL

WALK 3

6 miles (9½ km). Old field paths, minor roads and panoramic views.

By bus: There are buses from Huddersfield, Leeds, Dewsbury, Bradford and Wakefield to Mirfield. Get off at the Library and walk down Station Road.

By train: There are trains from Huddersfield, Dewsbury, Leeds and Wakefield to Mirfield on the Huddersfield line. Leave the station and walk up Station Road towards the centre of Mirfield, cross the canal and turn left down to the towpath.

By car: Park in Mirfield Library car park (pay-and-display). Walk down Station Road.

Stile near Bog Hall

Walk down Station Road and at the canal turn right along the towpath. Pass Mirfield Boat Yard and Ledgard Flood Lock and go under the bridge, then turn right up the ramp and through the gate and right again to cross the bridge over the canal. Go under the railway and over the river bridge, turn right again and take the middle road at the junction (Chadwick Lane). Pass to the left of Hopton School and enter the new housing estate. Take the first street on the right (Chadwick Hall Gardens), but in 20 yards turn left up a tarmac drive which leads to a kissing-gate beside a large gate. Go through and follow the wall on the right along through two fields. Pass through a stile and now follow the wall on your left. Cross a stile and follow the enclosed track to Boyfe Hall. Go through a stile by a gate into the garden, pass to the left of the house and walk up the drive, then left up the tarmac lane to a minor road (Wood Lane).

Turn right and walk along and then down the road, enjoying the view of Mirfield laid out on the right. Pass under the first railway bridge and then go left along Helme Lane. Follow the lane, bending left and then right to reach the B6118. Cross to the footway and turn left. Ignore the entrance to Bog Hall Farm on the left, but 40 yards further on cross the road and

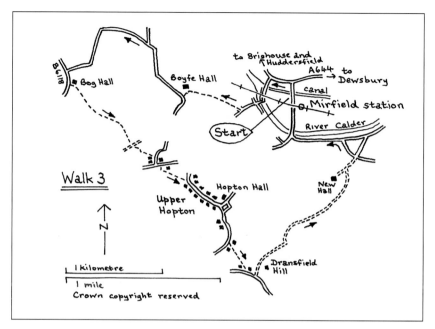

Walk 3

↑
N
|

1 Kilometre

1 mile

Crown copyright reserved

turn sharply left back along a narrow tarmac lane. In a few yards a footpath sign points right between a garage and a wall. Follow the path as it turns right, cross the stone stile at the end and turn left with the garden on the left to a stile in the wall ahead (there is a large gate on the left). Cross the stile and turn right to follow the wall on the right through two fields. At the next field go slightly left across the field to a stile in the wall just to the left of a large tree.

Pass through the stile and again go slightly left across the field to a stile at the right hand end of a clump of trees. Pass through the stile and aiming for the top of a metal pylon which you can just make out on the skyline walk up the field to a stile in the wall. Cross North Moor Lane, go through the stile opposite and head slightly left to a gate in the corner of the field. Go through the stile by the gate, then continue uphill in the same direction (there are panoramic views) and go around the wall corner to a stile into North Gate. Turn right along the lane past cottages, and at the main road (Hollin Hall Lane) turn left for some 50 yards, go through a gap in the wall on the right, walk forward to cross a track and continue up an enclosed way to a gate. Go through the gate and turn left with a hedge on the right as far as a stile in it, cross and turn left with the wall now on the left. Follow it to the main road (Jackroyd Lane).

15

Turn right up the road into Upper Hopton, passing a cricket field on the left. At the road junction continue straight ahead (it is worth going left for a look at Hopton Old Hall), past the school on the right and uphill. Where the road bends right, cross and fork left down a track on the left of a terrace

Hopton Old Hall

of stone houses. When the track bends left, keep forward to a stile, and then head across the field to some buildings on the skyline. Pass between houses and barn into Liley Lane.

Turn left along the road and take the first track on the left (bridleway sign), and where the track bears right go through the gate ahead (more panoramic views - you are now on Dransfield Hill) and then downhill with wall, hedge and fence on the left. Near the bottom of the field, when the fence turns left, go with it, passing between hawthorns, on a clear path which soon bears right to a stile by a gate. Cross the stile and go half right down the field to a gate, go through the gate and follow a rough track across the middle of the next field. Go through a gate and keep forward. After a time you have an old hedge on the left and you reach another gate. (Walk 4 comes down the steps on the right.)

Cross the stile by the gate and continue along the track. Cross another stile, but where the track bends left to Newhall Farm, go through the **small** gate on the right and turn left on the hedged path. On reaching the farm access road, turn right down it. At the road junction turn left and at the T-junction at Granny Lane left again. At Hopton New Road turn right over the bridge (River Calder) and walk up Station Road to the starting point.

LADY WOOD AND WHITLEY WOOD

WALK 4

4¼ miles (7 km). The most beautiful walk in the book, an exploration of the woodland south of the Calder. But this is not flat countryside, and there are ups and downs, although this way round the downs are steeper than the ups. Some sections may be excessively muddy.

By bus: There are buses from Huddersfield, Leeds, Dewsbury, Bradford and Wakefield to Mirfield. Get off at the Library and walk down Station Road.

By train: There are trains from Huddersfield, Dewsbury, Leeds and Wakefield to Mirfield on the Huddersfield line. Leave the station and walk up Station Road towards the centre of Mirfield, and at the canal turn right down to the towpath.

By car: Park in the car park behind Mirfield Library (pay-and-display).

Walk down Station Road, cross the canal bridge, turn left along the towpath and follow this to the lock at Shepley Bridge. Cross the bridge over the canal to the road, then turn right over the bridge across the river Calder. Turn left into the car park of the Ship Inn, walk straight across it and continue along a

Shepley Lock

paved track. Deep wheel ruts in the paving stones testify to much use in earlier times. Follow the path along the river bank. At a fork keep right on the clearer, ascending path, then turn left alongside the railway. Cross the railway bridge and keep straight ahead through the barrier into Lady Wood.

Where the track begins to bend right and a line of large stones across the path marks where a beck crosses it, go through the gap in the fence on the left, immediately turn left, with an old wall on your right, climb through some scattered stone foundations and turn right on a broad path. Now you must follow any one of various good paths straight up to the top edge of the wood. Don't get too far to the right, or you'll meet

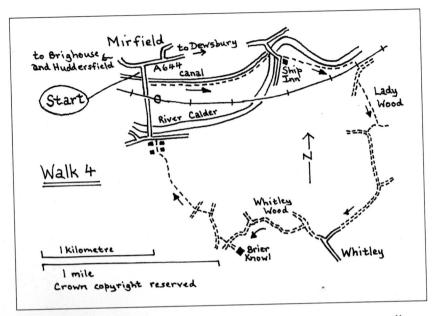

Walk 4

1 Kilometre

1 mile
Crown copyright reserved

the track again. (If you would like a more precise route, walk up through the wood until a deep ditch crosses the path. Cross it and in a few yards turn left on a clear cross path. At a fork keep left, i.e. straight on, and in a few yards you are joined by another path coming in from the left. Keep on your path, soon walking about 40 yards in from the left hand edge of the wood, and it will lead you to a stile in the top edge of the wood.)

At the top of the wood cross a stile into a field and keep forward up the old hedgerow. The hill on the right is an old spoil heap from the days when there were many small coal pits in the area. When you reach a cross path at an old stone gatepost, turn right, still along an old field boundary. At the end of the field the path bends left, with a fence on the right, and in 40 yards passes through a gap-stile to reach a cross-track by another old gatepost. Turn left.

Follow this old packhorse track (Hunger Hill Lane), one of the loveliest in the area, with its causey stones and with Jordan Wood on the right. The path climbs, levels out, then climbs again. You now have Dewsbury & District golf course on the right. Some sections of the path may be almost impassable because of mud. At a junction fork right on a path climbing more steeply. When the track levels out again at the top of the hill, Whitley Lower is across the fields on the left and there is a good

18

view over the golf course to Mirfield and beyond. When you reach the tarmac access lane to Whitley Water Treatment Works, keep forward along it, but where it turns left to Whitley village, turn right onto a track known as Mouse Hole Lane. After 200 yards fork left down a wide track which leads steeply downhill through Whitley Wood.

At the bottom cross the stile, walk down the lane, and fork left at the junction. When the road turns left up to a farm (Brier Knowl), fork right off it. Follow the track for a few yards then go through a kissing-gate on the right and follow the path downhill with the wall on the left. Go through a stile and another kissing-gate and bear right

Mouse Hole Lane

along the enclosed path. At the top of the hill go over a stile on the left and walk straight across the field to the stile on the far side. From here there is another fine view of Mirfield. Cross over a track (here you cross Walk 3) and follow the edge of the field straight downhill. At the bottom go over the footbridge over Valance Beck and a stile.

Follow the path across the field to the edge of the wood (Briery Bank). The path now follows the edge of the field, then cuts across a corner to a stile. Cross into a narrow path behind houses. At a track turn right, then after 25 yards left along another path. At a junction of paths turn right through a stone gap-stile to reach Granny Lane at Hopton Bottom. Cross the road and turn left, then right over the new river bridge on Hopton New Road to return to the starting point.

LILEY HALL, BLACK DICK'S TOWER, WHITLEY LOWER AND OUZELWELL HALL

WALK 5

5½ miles (8¾ km). A pleasant mix of field paths and old tracks, with some attractive woodland and good views.

By bus: 241 Huddersfield-Lepton-Grange Moor (hourly, no service evenings and Sundays) to the Hare & Hounds pub on Liley Lane (B6118); walk 100 yards further in the Grange Moor direction. Or 207/208 Dewsbury-Whitley-Grange Moor (hourly, Sundays it is the 210/211 two-hourly) to Quebec Farm, Whitley Road, and start the walk at [*].
By car: There is a large layby 120 yards on the Grange Moor side of the Hare & Hounds pub on Liley Lane (B6118). Park here.

The walk starts at the Liley Lane Works (the Moxon Group). Cross the road and go down the lane opposite as far as the right hand bend, where you go over the stile on the left and walk half left uphill to a fence corner on the right; keeping well to the right of a line of trees across the field, then follow the fence on the right along to a corner. Turn left, and then half left again and walk diagonally up the field to a stile in the wooden fence at the top. A good indicator is to make for a point to the right of Black Dick's Tower. Look back for a splendid panorama as you climb. *"Black Dick"* *was Sir Richard Beaumont (1574-1631), born in Whitley Hall,*

Black Dick's Tower

knighted by King James I in 1609 and MP in 1625. He sold off his estates to pay his gambling debts, had two illegitimate daughters, and was a highwayman (thus "Black Dick"). His ghost is said to walk from the Tower to the Hall (now demolished).

Cross the track and the stile and walk steeply uphill to the stile at the top of the bank. Cross straight over the field (more fine views) to a stone stile and sign at a road, turn right along the footway for about 100 yards, then cross the road and enter a signposted track. After a time the enclosed way bends left. Pass under one set of power lines (giant pylons!), but before you reach the next, cross a stile on the right and walk along the left hand edge of the field. You pass under the power lines again. In the bottom corner of the field turn right along the hedge until a large signposted gap is reached, turn left through the gap and follow the track down the field, soon parallel to trees on the right. Follow the track straight down through a farm and on to a road.

Turn left up the road. Ignore a footpath sign pointing right through the gates of a house and keep on up the footway until opposite the entrance to Falhouse Green Farm on the left you cross a stile by a gate on the right and walk along the right hand edge of the field. In the corner of the field go through the kissing-gate and continue now with the hedge on the left. In the next corner go through the gateway ahead and now the way is fenced. When you reach the corner of the churchyard wall, keep it on your right and follow it down to the road in Whitley.

Turn left up the road to a T-junction, then turn right down the main road as far as the second lot of buildings on the left (Quebec Farm) (about 50 yards after a brick chimney on the right hand side of the road). [*] Go through the little gate beside the main gate (signposted) and up the track. Pass to the left of the house, up the track to a stile on the left of a large wooden gate. Over the stile go slightly left up the next field to a stile by a gate at the top. Cross the stile and go fairly sharply left uphill to a stile beside a gate in the fence/wall at the top. Walk straight across the next field over the brow of the hill (Thornhill Edge is off to the right) to a stile at the right hand end of a very short section of broken wall. Pass through and keep forward down what used to be the right hand edge of the next field to a stile in the next corner, after which you are following a hedge on the left.

When the hedge ends, keep forward to drop to a paved track, turn left for a few yards to a junction, then go right along an enclosed track

Walk 5

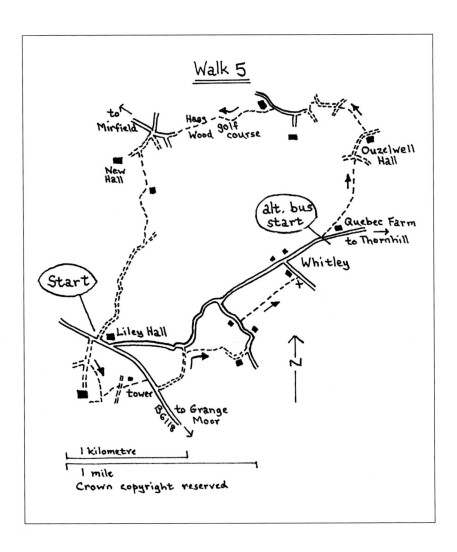

1 kilometre

1 mile

Crown copyright reserved

downhill towards Ouzelwell Hall. The track leads round to the left of the house, then you pass a large stone barn. At the end of this turn left down an enclosed track. Go through the gate at the bottom and continue with the hedge on your right to the trees at the bottom. Keep forward over the beck, then follow the hedge on the left up the next field to reach a track. Turn left along this, and almost immediately at the junction bear right. When the track bends right, fork left off it, i.e. keep straight ahead on a clear path along the right hand edge of a field.

At the far end of the field turn left, still along the field edge, for 50 yards, to reach a track on a bend. Bear right here. On reaching a tarmac lane keep forward along it. When you reach the next group of houses (marked on the map as Calder Farm), fork left at the first opportunity, cross the stile by the gate ahead and walk up the right hand edge of the field to a stile at the corner of the wood. Drop into the narrow walled footpath and follow it to Dewsbury District Golf Course. Walk straight forward across two fairways (the first playing from the right, the second from the left), then keep forward through the trees to reach a cross track.

Turn right downhill through the wood. At the foot ignore a gate ahead and turn left through a gateway into Hagg Wood, cross the beck and follow the broad contouring path through the wood, which you leave through an old gateway into a walled lane. Follow this down, and when the tarmac surface begins, keep forward along it. The road broadens and you reach a junction. On the right is a post box, on the left are two access roads. Take the second of these (bridleway sign) to New Hall Farm.

When the track forks, keep left (New Hall Farm is up to the right) along the path between hedges. After a time it passes to the right of the cluster of houses at Royds House. When you approach the valley bottom, ignore a path forking left through a gate, and soon you have a beck on the right for a short distance. A wall starts on the right: follow it up to a gate ahead, go through and bear right with the wall and Gregory Spring Wood on your right. Follow the track to Liley Hall, through the farmyard and out to Liley Lane and your starting point. (Bus walkers who started at Quebec Farm will now cross the road and jump to the start of the walk description.)

KIRKHEATON, LEPTON AND HALL WOOD

WALK 6

5 miles (8 km). Pleasant field paths and old tracks through undulating pastoral countryside, with fine views.

By bus: 241 Huddersfield-Lepton-Grange Moor (hourly, no service evenings and Sundays) to the junction of Healey Green Lane and Liley Lane (B6118).
By car: There is a large layby 120 yards on the Grange Moor side of the Hare & Hounds pub on Liley Lane (B6118). Park here and walk along the footway past the Hare & Hounds to where a minor road, Healey Green Lane, forks left.

Walk along Healey Green Lane, then take the first farm access road on the right. On reaching Lower Stone Royd Farm the track turns left to pass to the left of the buildings and end at a stile by a gate. Cross and follow the wall on the right towards Hutchin Wood. Cross the stile in the corner and continue by the fence and wood on the left. Cross another stile in the next corner and keep on by the wood, ignoring a stile into it. When the wood ends, turn right and keep the fence/hedge on your left to a stile in the next corner.

Walk forward, cross a track to a stile beyond, then keep forward with a fence on the right to a stile in a brick wall, then keep on between wall and hedge to a stile into a field. Bear slightly left across the field to a stile in a broken wall, then follow the same line over the next field to a stile just to the left of a telegraph pole. Walk downhill with a wall on the left to the field corner, then turn right and continue down the left hand edge of the field. In the bottom corner turn left and follow a clear path down to reach steps and a bridge over a beck. Bear left and follow the clear path up to a field.

Walk straight across to the hedge opposite and turn right, with the hedge on your left and a huge quarry below. Look out for a point where the path bears left to pass through bracken. After a time the clear contouring path climbs slightly and bears right. Ignore a path forking left downhill here and keep forward into the remains of a walled lane. At the end of this pass through a wide gap on the left, then follow a hedge on the right down, after a time picking up a fence on the left, to a tarmac lane.

Turn right along it and follow it as it bends left to a T-junction. You are now in Kirkheaton. Cross and turn left for 25 yards to find a gap-stile on the right which is just to the left of the entrance gate to houses 10/12.

Follow the paved path to the next road and cross to the track opposite. When you are faced by a gate, go through the stile on the right, turn sharp left for a few yards, cross another stile on the left, turn sharp right and resume your original direction! Cross the bridge and keep forward into an enclosed path which climbs to a stile into a field. Keep straight forward up the field, cross a stile by a gate and continue by a wall on the right, passing three old stone gateposts.

Cross the stile at the top (the building on the left is a cricket pavilion) and follow the wall on the left. Cross the stile and the access lane to the cricket field, another stile, then follow the wall on the right up the field, bearing slightly left near the top to the next stile. Walk half left over the next field to the next stile, but instead of crossing it, turn right and follow the field edge to another stile in the corner. Continue along the left hand edge of the next field. Go through the stile in the corner and walk half left over the next field to a stile beside three trees, then straight over the next field to a stile on the left of a gate. Turn right up the road (Gawthorpe Lane).

On reaching the junction with Highfield Lane, turn left along a rough track (Thurgory Lane) and follow it for about a mile until you are about

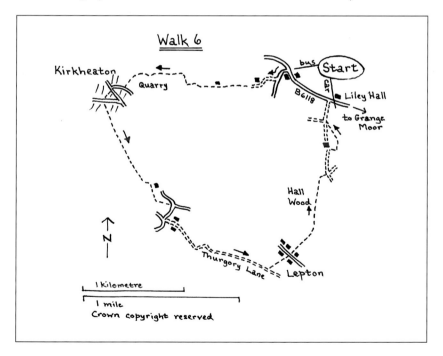

100 yards from the houses of Croft House. Here cross a wooden stile on the left, at the end of a section of hedge, and walk slightly right over the field to the stile opposite. Walk down the right hand edge of the next field, cross the stile and walk down the track to the next road. You are now in Lepton. Cross and turn left for about 10 yards, then right into a walled footpath. When it ends, continue down the left hand edge of the field to the next stile, then go slightly left down the middle of the next very large field to the trees at the bottom.

Cross the stile and footbridge and bear left along the path through Hall Wood. On the far side you reach a junction of tracks. Turn left. When the lane ends at the entrance into a large house (The Kennels), cross the stile on the right into an enclosed path. At the end turn right through a kissing-gate and walk up the field with a fence on the left. Go through another kissing-gate by a pair of old stone gateposts and turn left, still with the fence on your left. At the next corner, where the fence again turns left, walk half left down the field, keeping well to the left of the pylon, to a stile near a cattle-grid. Bear right along the track to the B6118. Here drivers will find their cars, and from here buses return to Huddersfield.

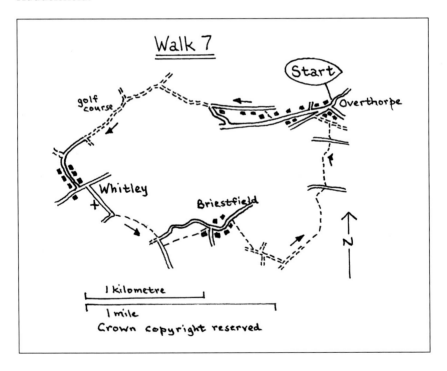

26

WHITLEY AND BRIESTFIELD

WALK 7

4¼ miles (6¾ km). A pleasant walk with three villages, three pubs, a few steep bits, but plenty of good views. Some sections can be very muddy.

By bus: 207/208 Dewsbury-Whitley bus (hourly; Sun 2-hourly as 210/211) to a bus stop on an island in the road, just before the Black Horse Inn, Edge Top Road.
By car: Take the road out of Dewsbury for Thornhill and follow the signs for Whitley, forking right into Overthorpe Road. After 3 miles look out for a bus stop on an island on the left of the road and beside it turn into the dual carriageway with a broad strip of grass in the centre. There is plenty of room to park here. It is a short distance before the Black Horse Inn.

Continue up Edge Top Road to pass the Black Horse on your right, ignore Briestfield Road forking left and walk along Whitley Road past Edge Top Working Men's Club on the right, then the Baptist Chapel on the left. About 30 yards past a bus stop, at a cobbled drive, turn right up a steep fenced path through a wood.

Turn left on reaching Foxroyd Lane. There are good views of the Calder Valley on the right and Emley Moor on the left. Where the road begins to descend, passes a house and bends sharply to the left, keep straight forward along a track with causey stones in the middle. At the end of the wood on the right the track veers right. Where the track turns right again to Ouzelwell Hall, keep forward along a footpath with the remains of causey stones. This is Back Lane, which can be very muddy.

At the next T-junction by a holly tree turn left uphill. After a time there is a golf course on the right (Dewsbury & District Golf Club). When you reach a tarmac road, keep forward along it. It takes you into Whitley. Walk through the village and turn left at the Woolpack Inn. In a short distance turn right into Howroyd Lane. Pass Whitley Church. Where the road turns right, cross the stile straight ahead and walk down the left hand edge of the field on a concrete path. Cross a stile into woodland and continue downhill. At the bottom cross the beck by a footbridge and go up a partly cobbled, partly flagged path to a stile and the Briestfield Road, which you reach on a bend. Go straight forward on the road for 90 yards, pass through a small gate on the left (signposted) and walk straight across the field.

Follow the slight ridge past a concrete trough, pass the old stile at the end of a wall to reach a stile 10 yards to the right of a gate. Cross another field to a stile on the left of a metal gate, then bear half left and right round the end of a building and follow the wall on the right to a stile and a road. Turn right into Briestfield and left at the Shoulder of Mutton. After 180 yards cross a signposted stile on the right and walk along a short stretch of enclosed path. Go through a gate and walk down the right hand edge of the field. Cross a stile, go down the stone steps and down the grass to pass to the right of the house and of a large tree, cross a stile and reach a track. Turn left.

Cross the beck and at the next fork keep right uphill. A short distance further up keep left at another fork up an old walled lane. At the T-junction turn left on a green lane (Sowood Lane; here you join the Kirklees Way), at the end of which cross the stile and keep forward down the hill with the remains of a wall on your right. At the end of the field keep forward down through the trees, soon bearing left to cross the beck by a footbridge. Go forward with the beck on your right, at the end of the field bearing right, then turning sharp left after the end of the hedge to a stile. Walk up the field to a ladder-stile at the top, then follow the hedge on the left and pass through a gateway in the top corner. Follow the fence on the left, ignore the stile by the gate, and bear right to follow the wall on your left up to a stile by a metal gate.

Cross straight over the tarmac lane to the stile opposite and follow the wall on your left to a stile by a gate. Continue downhill, keeping the hedge to your right, near the bottom of the field entering a path between hedges, which leads to a footbridge. Cross and follow the track up to Low Road. Turn left for 20 yards to a signposted footpath on the right. At the time of writing, building works are in progress up here, but essentially the path leads straight up to the next road. At present, when you reach a track, keep up it for a few yards, soon with a new paling fence on the right, and where this bends right, look out for the continuation of the narrow path straight ahead, which can be overgrown. At the next street turn left, but immediately after house 138 on the right, climb a flight of steps. At the top turn left to Briestfield Road, then right to return to the Black Horse and the start of the walk.

AROUND GRANGE MOOR

WALK 8

7 miles (11¾ km). A particularly pleasant round, typical of this countryside. Many ups and downs, with panoramic views. An attractive selection of old lanes, and some nice properties.

By bus: 231/232 Huddersfield-Emley-Wakefield (half-hourly Mon-Sat, hourly Sun) to the Dartmouth Arms pub on Paul Lane near Linfit Lane Top and start the walk at [*].

By car: A quarter of a mile on the Wakefield side of of the Kaye Arms public house on the A642 Wakefield to Huddersfield road at Grange Moor (GR 232 156) there is a walled lane on the north side of the road (Denby Grange Lane) and a layby opposite it. Park here.

Two footpaths leave the layby at stiles. Cross the right hand stile (immediately to the left of a gate) and follow the hedge on the left through two fields. At the end of the second cross a stone step-stile, turn left along the wall and follow it round and down to the bottom corner of the field. A short ginnel leads to the main road in Flockton. Cross diagonally right and take the street opposite. Where it bends left, cross a stile on the right and walk down the field with the fence on your left. Where the fence ends, keep straight down to the bottom right hand corner of the field. Cross the beck by the stone bridge and follow the fence on the right along the front of the house to a stile in the corner. Cross and turn left up the access drive.

On reaching a T-junction, turn right and follow the track (Common Lane) to Six Lanes End. Cross the road and take the track to the left of the terrace of houses. At Crows Nest, the farm at the top of the hill, turn left, but where the walled track bends right, keep forward along the top edge of the field with a wall/hedge on the right. Cross a stile and follow the wall to Cockermouth Farm. Go through a kissing-gate, cross a track and two stiles, go through the large gate on the right and resume your direction, now with the fence on your left. Go through another kissing-gate and bear half-left over the next field to another kissing-gate beside a large metal gate. Turn right along the farm road, but just before you reach the next farm cross a stile on the left and walk half-right down the field to the next stile, then keep your direction to the next stile and a road. Turn right.

Pass the Beaconsfield Gallery and the Dartmouth Arms. [*] At the end of the houses cross the stile on the left and walk half-right down the field,

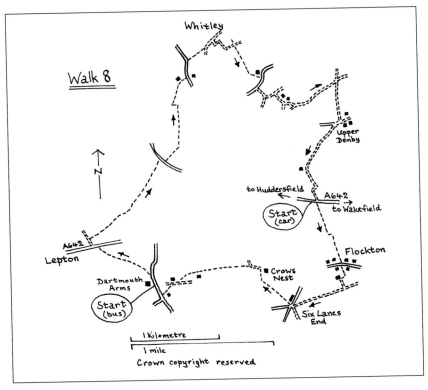

Walk 8

Whitley

Upper Denby

to Huddersfield
A642
to Wakefield
Start (car)

Flockton

Lepton
A642

Dartmouth Arms

Start (bus)

Crows Nest

Six Lanes End

1 Kilometre

1 mile

Crown copyright reserved

enjoying splendid views. Cross the next stile and follow a clear narrow path up through dense gorse. Go through a metal kissing-gate and bear half-left over the next enormous field. After you breast the rise, make for the right hand end of playing fields, where you will find another kissing-gate. Go through and follow the right hand edge of the playing fields to the A642 on the edge of Lepton. Cross and turn right past the White Horse.

Take the first farm access road on the left through a wood. At the end of the wood cross the stile on the right and keeping a wall and then a fence on your right drop down to cross two stiles 35 yards apart and a beck. Follow the hedge on your left round and up to the next (double) stile and keep on with the hedge/fence to your left. When the fence goes left keep straight on to a gap-stile near the right hand corner of the wood. Walk straight up to the next stile at the top of the slope. Bear slightly left across the next field to a stile in the top corner. With the wall on your left (there are fine views over it) continue past a gateway on the left to a stile by a gate. Now you have a wood on your left (Grange Moor is over to the right), but where it curves left keep straight on along the wallside to a stile by a gate.

Turn right along the road for 80 yards to a stile by a gate on the left. Walk down with the hedge on your left. About 20 yards before the end of the field there is a stile on the left. Cross and follow the fence on your right to the next stile. Cross and bear slightly right across the middle of the very large field. Pass through the remains of a fence and continue down the middle of the next field as far as a large white notice. Here turn sharp left down to the fence corner at the wood. Go through the kissing-gate into the wood a few yards down from the corner and follow the path contouring through the wood with a steep drop to your left. Emerge from the wood by crossing a fence, cross a very wet patch of rough ground by a boardwalk, to pick up a fence on your right leading to a house. Cross a stile in the wall ahead and walk down the track to reach the road by a stile.

Turn left. The road bends right, but where it bends left again, fork right off it down a bridleway. The causey stones indicate the former importance of this route. Where the path widens, ignore a farm road on the right, enjoy the view up to Whitley Church and take the next track on the right. It winds uphill and bends left. When you reach a point with a stile on each side of the track, cross the one on the right – a few steps lead up to it – and bear slightly left uphill, where the next stile soon appears. Cross it and walk straight across the next field to the next stile, then follow the fence on the left up (more panoramic views), cross the stile in the top corner – two in quick succession – and follow the hedge on the left down past Dale Green Farm to a stile and the Briestfield Road.

Turn right. Take the first track on the left (a No Through Road), keep left at the fork, then take the next track on the right. Drop to cross a beck – there are some fine houses around here – ignore the next track on the right and keep forward to climb to a T-junction. Turn left. At the next crossing of tracks turn sharp right and follow this track up to the houses of Upper Denby, a charming hamlet. Bear right, then immediately fork left along Denby Grange Lane, which you follow to the A642. Here motorists will find their cars, and bus walkers should jump to the start of the walk description to continue their way.

FLOCKTON, NEW HALL AND MIDDLESTOWN

WALK 9

7½ miles (12 km). Attractive, but undulating countryside, so there are lots of ups and downs. But the walking is easy, largely on tracks and old lanes, with some field paths.

By bus: 231/232 Huddersfield-Wakefield (Mon-Sat half-hourly) (Sun 232 hourly), 128/129 Dewsbury-Overton-Horbury-Wakefield (Mon-Sat 20/40 mins; no service evenings and Sun), to the White Swan in Middlestown.
By car: On the A637 Huddersfield-Barnsley road, about halfway between Flockton Green and the Black Bull Inn, there is a tall water tower, and about 200 yards from this in the Barnsley direction there is a long layby. Park here, cross the road and walk along the footway towards the water tower, but before you reach it cross a stile on the right and start the walk at [*] below.

The walk starts at the White Swan in the centre of Middlestown. Go straight across the main road and along Thornhill Road. After about 200 yards turn left along Nell Gap Lane for about 100 yards then right into an enclosed footpath. Where it ends, keep forward on a clear path through the wood. The path joins a broader track. Near the end of the wood ignore the track straight ahead and turn sharp right on a clear narrow path with a wooden fence to the left. There is a fine view of Thornhill Edge. Descend some steps and cross a stile on the left. Walk straight over the field, cutting the corner on the right, to a stile in the facing hedge. Keep on the same line through two more fields to a stile into a small wood and walk through the wood to a stile on the far side. Keep forward along the track, ignoring tracks to left and right.

The track ends at a gate into Mug Mill Farm: here turn right down a rough path, cross a footbridge over Smithy Brook and walk up the lane towards Thornhill Edge. At the top of the lane cross the road and turn left for about 40 yards, then right up an old cobbled way (it starts as tarmac), known locally as Fanny Hill, to the Flatt Top Hotel. Turn left and follow Albion Road downhill. Ignore Edge Road on the left, and keep left at the fork along Low Road. After the last bungalow (no.9) turn left down a narrow path between walls. Keep straight on along the high banked lane (which could be in Devon). Bear right at the T-junction and in a few yards fork left down the lane which drops to cross Smithy Brook again. On the skyline to the left is the National Mining Museum.

Do not enter the grounds of Heigh House, but follow the track round to

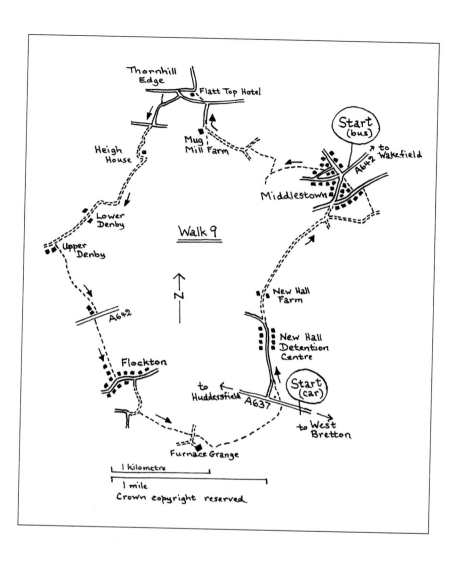

Thornhill Edge
Flatt Top Hotel
Heigh House
Mug Mill Farm
Start (bus)
to Wakefield
A642
Middlestown
Lower Denby
Walk 9
Upper Denby
N
New Hall Farm
A642
New Hall Detention Centre
Flockton
to Huddersfield A637
Start (car)
to West Bretton
Furnace Grange

1 Kilometre
1 mile
Crown copyright reserved

33

the right, then the left, to bypass it. The track bends right again and begins to ascend. It is joined by another track from the right, broadens and soon swings right towards a bungalow, where it turns left to pass the farm buildings of Lower Denby. The road, now roughly surfaced, keeps uphill and there are views of Briestfield on its ridge and the tower of Whitley Church. The track levels out and approaches Upper Denby.

Across the track is a large gate with a small one beside it. Go through and immediately turn left over a stile by another gate. Here you join the Kirklees Way. Negotiate three more stiles and walk down the slope with the wall on your right. Cross a stile in this wall and keep on downhill. Cross another stile and the bridge over the beck and follow the clear path up through the wood.

Join a track for a short distance, but when it curves sharp left, keep forward past the end of a wall. Leave the wood and keep forward to cross a stile by a gate in the wall ahead, then follow the right hand edge of the next field. Cross a stile into an enclosed path, pass through a turnstile gate near a house and walk past the front of the houses up to the Huddersfield-Wakefield road. Turn right for 50 yards, then cross the road to the signposted stile opposite and follow the right hand edge of the field to a stile. Now follow the fence on the left. The path leads all the way to the main road in Flockton.

Turn left past the former Methodist Chapel and Hill Top Road, then take the broad lane on the right opposite the bus stop. It soon becomes a track. The tower of Emley Church is prominent ahead. At the bottom turn left onto another track over the beck, then left again, to walk between the back of a house and the beck, turning right past the end of the house and over a stile. Turn left and follow the beck, but when it turns sharp left, keep straight forward up the slope and you will soon see a stile in the fence/hedge ahead. Cross and walk forward for about 10 yards, then the path forks slightly right across the field, heading to the left of the farm in the distance (Furnace Grange). Cross the stile on the far side of the field and walk straight across the next field to the next stile, crossing a concrete track just before you reach it.

Keep forward over the next field with the farm on the right, cross the stile in the next hedge, and keep forward to the right of the hedge. Just past two oak trees turn left over a stile (here leaving the Kirklees Way) and walk straight over the field. On the far side bear right with the beck to your left until you can cross it by a footbridge. Walk up with the fence on your left, soon up the left hand edge of a very large field. After about 150 yards, where the hedge makes a slight bulge into the field, the right of way forks right across the field, heading for the second of three trees to the right of a derelict barn. On reaching the hedge/wall at the top of the field, turn left to pass between the wall and the barn, and when the hedge ends, keep forward to the left of a line of trees to the Barnsley-Huddersfield road. Motorists will find their cars a short distance to the right, otherwise cross the road diagonally left to a stile.

[*] Drop diagonally left down the field to a stile in the bottom corner. Go left for a yard or two to a tarmac lane and turn right down it. Walk straight through the grounds of New Hall Detention Centre to the far side. At the end of the houses, where the road swings left, keep straight on on a narrower lane. Follow this straight through between the buildings of New Hall Farm and keep on until you reach a T-junction. Here turn right and in a few yards keep left at the fork and follow Chapel Hill Lane down towards Middlestown.

Immediately after a cottage turn right for a few yards, then left. Follow the track past farm buildings on the right and through a gateway. Soon you have an open field on the left. About 100 yards after an old footpath sign in the hedge on the right (easily missed) fork left up a narrow path towards the trees. Go up a flight of brick steps and follow the hedge on the left towards the houses. Views of Horbury and Wakefield appear on the right. The path leads up between two houses to the road. Cross and turn left for 50 yards, then right along a signposted path which leads back to the crossroads in Middlestown. If you have timed your arrival well, the White Swan and the Little Bull will provide refreshment at the end of your walk. Motorists will now jump to the start of the walk description.

THORNHILL EDGE AND DIMPLEDALE

WALK 10

5½ miles (9 km). A varied walk along field paths and old tracks, with panoramic views. There are several ups and downs, which makes the walk more strenuous than the distance might suggest. There are toilets at the start.

By bus: 128/129 Dewsbury-Wakefield (20/40 minutes, not evenings or Sundays), 207/208 Dewsbury-Whitley (hourly; Sun 2-hourly as 210/211), 281 Dewsbury-Thornhill Edge (10 minutes, half-hourly evenings and Sundays), to Frank Lane (Church Lane end).
By car: Park in Thornhill Rectory car park in Church Lane.

Leave the car park by the lodge, cross the road, go up the steps and turn left into Valley Road. At the end of the metalled road keep forward along a broad track. Descend through a gully, and when a brick wall starts on the left, fork right on a path keeping about the same height. In 20 yards at the next fork keep right again, on a narrow path which contours along a short distance below the top of Thornhill Edge. There are fine views left over the valley of Smithy Brook.

About 15 yards after passing a stone post with a wooden marker post beside it a paved path comes in from the right. Go half left here down a clear path through gorse bushes to a road. Turn right along the road for 40 yards, then turn sharp left down a tarmac access road and follow it to the valley bottom. Here fork left off the track over a footbridge over Smithy Beck and follow an enclosed path, which passes to the left of Mug Mill Farm. When a track comes in from the left, keep forward up an old hedged way, which after a time is still causeyed. The path leads to a stile: cross it and walk straight over the field to another stile and a narrow road.

On Thornhill Edge

Turn right down the lane, with views of Thornhill Edge. At the bottom of the hill where the lane turns right, leave the road and keep straight on over a stile by a gate. Keep up the farm track, crossing another stile, but when it turns left to Hazle Greave Farm keep forward on another track which after a time crosses a little beck. Cross the stile by the gate a few yards ahead and walk up a sunken lane to a stile into the wood.

The clear path follows the wall on the right before bearing left through the wood. Cross a track diagonally left and follow the path down to a bridge over a beck. Cross the stile in the wall ahead and turn sharp right across the field to a stile onto a track. Turn left up it. It soon bends left by a house. After about 20 yards look for a stile on the right. Walk straight across the field to pick up a hedge/fence on the right.

Now follow a clear track down to a dip, crossing a stile by a gate, and walk up the other side with a wall/fence on the left to a stile. Keep forward up the left hand edge of the next field to reach a cross track (Sowood Lane). Cross the track and go straight ahead along a broad track down to Dimpledale. Near the foot you are joined by a better track from the left. Ignore a track forking right, cross the beck and turn right into the access drive to a cottage. But immediately cross a stile on the left, walk over the grass and climb steeply to a stile in the fence at the top. Walk straight up the left hand edge of the next field. In the top corner cross a stile into a short enclosed path which leads to the road in Briestfield.

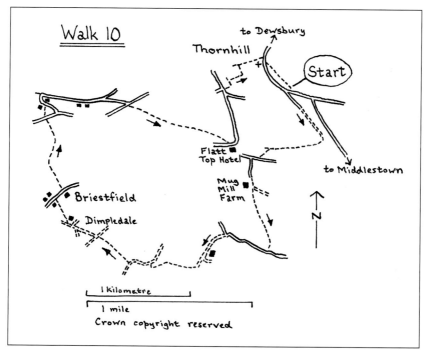

Cross the road, turn right and follow the footway for 100 yards. Cross the stile on the left beside a gate opposite Wilson House Farm and walk down with the wall on the left to a stile, then with the wall on the right to the next (double) stile. Keep the fence/wall on the right, but where the fence turns sharp right, keep forward to a stile in the bottom corner of the field. Over this, keep forward with the wall on the right until it turns sharp right, at which point go half right to pass between the end of an old wall and a small wood, then keep on downhill parallel to the shallow valley on the right and follow it all the way down to the trees at the bottom. Pass the remains of an old stone stile and cross a wooden footbridge. Cross the stile and walk forward for a short distance, then bear right and then left to follow the fence/hedge on the right up (ignoring a stile near a gate in it) to a stile in the top corner of the field. Keep forward, soon again with a hedge on the right, which you follow up to a stile and Whitley Road.

Cross to the footway opposite, turn right, and after 30 yards cross the wall on the left (footpath sign) and walk up the left hand edge of the field to a stile in the top left hand corner. Turn left up the tarmac lane (Jackson Lane) and follow it as it turns right. Wide views, urban and rural, appear on both sides of the ridge. At the Council estate take the first road on the right and at the end follow the paved footpath to the end of Foxroyd Lane. Turn right, cross the main road (Whitley Road), and turn left, in a few yards go down the steps on the right, cross Briestfield Road into the tarmac drive opposite and keep straight ahead on the path along Thornhill Edge, a splendid panoramic walk.

Follow this path, which contours a short distance below the top of the Edge, until with Flatt Top Hotel a short distance ahead you must keep right at a fork and drop to a road. Turn left past the pub and follow the road round to the left past Thornhill Edge post office. Keep along the road (Edge Lane) to the Scarborough Hotel and turn right along the right hand edge of the hotel car park, continue forward along the footpath and at the T-junction turn left. After 40 yards turn right down a paved path, cross the road and keep down the paved path opposite.

When the paved path ends, keep forward between high hedges, but when you reach the corner of the churchyard on the left, turn left, keeping the churchyard wall on your right. When this wall turns right, stay with it and follow the church boundary all the way to the road at Church Lane, passing the 15th-century Thornhill Church on the way. As sharp bends restrict the view, cross with care, turn right for a short distance, then opposite the east end of the church go through an opening on the left and down some steps into Rectory Park. The building below is the Old Rectory, now an old people's home. Immediately turn right along the unsurfaced track parallel to the wall on the right, which leads through the park and back to the car park. Another gap in the wall on the right gives access to the nearest bus stop.

BY THE CALDER & HEBBLE NAVIGATION TO THORNHILL EDGE

WALK 11

6½ miles (10½ km). The Calder & Hebble Navigation links the Aire & Calder Navigation at Wakefield to Sowerby Bridge, a distance of 21½ miles. A long stretch of river and canalside walking, using the fine new towpath built by British Waterways, is followed by the long, steady climb to Edge Top, from where there are extensive views to north and south, and the gentle descent through attractive countryside back to the Calder valley. The route passes three pubs. The walk starts at Ravensthorpe Station.

By train: **There are trains from Huddersfield, Dewsbury, Leeds and Wakefield to Ravensthorpe on the Huddersfield line.**
By car: **There is room to park at Ravensthorpe Station.**

Walk up the station access road and turn right at the top. A few yards before the bridge over the Calder turn right down a cobbled path to the river and right again along the towpath. When you reach a barrage across the river and Thornhill Flood Gate the towpath changes sides. From here you follow the fine new towpath by the Calder & Hebble Navigation, passing the Perseverance pub, but seeing very little of Thornhill Lees, all the way to Double Locks and the junction with the canal branch to Dewsbury. Cross the bridge over this branch and bear right down to the towpath along the Long Cut. At the next lock cross the canal by the bridge and take the path straight ahead up towards the woods.

The path soon bends right and climbs gently. When you reach a concrete track, turn right down it. About 50 yards before you reach a gateway ahead, fork left on a narrow path (easily missed), partly cobbled, which climbs steeply and soon bends left, with a shallow valley on the right, to reach a metal fence. Follow this up, the path becoming enclosed, to a works forecourt, walk straight over this, up some steps and along a short ginnel to a road. A few yards to the left is the Alma Inn, your second pub. Cross and go up the street opposite, keeping to the paved footway. It bends left and leads steeply up to another street. Turn right. To the right there is a view to Dewsbury.

At the road junction at the top (The Cross) cross straight over - notice the old fountain on the left - and go up the road opposite, but in a few yards at the T-junction turn left. Overthorpe Road becomes Edge Top Road. Now follows the only dull stretch on the walk. At the top of the hill, just past the Black Horse, (the third and last pub) ignore a road forking left downhill, but a few yards further on cross the end of Foxroyd Lane on the right, go up the steps and along the paved path.

You are on the top of Thornhill Edge, and there is an extensive view left. When the paving ends, keep forward along the street, and at the road junction keep left. At the end of the reservoir wall on the right there is an extensive view over the Calder valley.

At the end of the houses the road begins to descend and after one last detached house it curves sharp left: keep straight ahead here along a paved track. In 50 yards, immediately before the wood starts on the right, fork right down some steps into an enclosed footpath. Cross a stile and continue down the right hand edge of two fields, then turn right down the farm road (Ouzelwell Lane). Pass a lane on the right leading to a large redbrick house, but take the next unsurfaced track forking left. In 50 yards ignore a track forking right. The large farm you pass is Crow Royd.

Some way after the farm you pass under three sets of power lines. A few yards after the third, a hedge comes in from the left and the track forks: keep right. Where the track ends, ignore a clear path forking right and keep along the right hand edge of the field, bending left at the end with a fence on the right. In 40 yards go through a stile and bear right along the track. At the end of the fence on the right fork right down a double paved track. Pass through a barrier into Lady Wood and follow the track all the way down to another barrier out of the wood. Ignore the railway bridge straight ahead and turn right along a track. At the end cross the road and turn left over the railway bridge then right down the station access road.

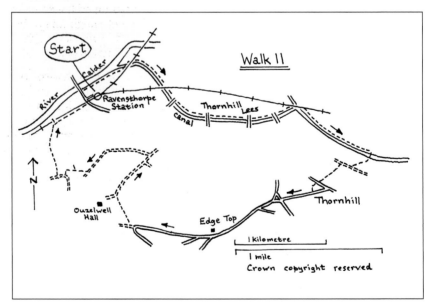

EMLEY AND FLOCKTON

WALK 12

4¼ miles (7 km). Very easy walking on old tracks and field paths through pleasant, undulating countryside. The route includes a short section of Kirklees Way. A short section of the walk coincides with the 3-mile Emley Village Trail. The route passes three old farms with the word "Grange" in their names, indicating monastic ownership in the Middle Ages, and the name "Furnace Grange" indicates one of the main activities of the monks - smelting iron from local bell pits.

By bus: 231/232 Huddersfield-Wakefield (half-hourly Mon-Sat, hourly Sun), 233 Huddersfield-Flockton (very infrequent, none on Sun), 934 link from Denby Dale Station (hourly, none on Sundays).

By car: Park in the car-park behind the post office which is beside the stump of the village cross in Emley village.

Start at Emley Cross (*the remains of the Market Cross - Emley was granted a royal charter in 1253 to hold a weekly market. The upper part of the cross was destroyed in the Civil War*) and with your back to Church Street turn right down the main road (Beaumont Street) for some 150 yards, and immediately before the White Horse Inn fork right down Outlane. After about ½ mile keep straight on at a crossing of tracks near Crawshaw Cottage, and after a further ½ mile you meet Haigh Lane, the road from Flockton to Emley Moor, at Six Lanes End. Turn sharp right along a rough lane for another ½ mile into Flockton Common End.

Shortly after the tarmac surface starts, just past a row of stone houses on the left, bear right at the junction (going left would take you to the centre of Flockton). When this lane peters out at a stone bridge on the left, keep forward along the footpath for 20 yards to find an enclosed path on the right. Follow this to a stile into a field and carry on straight ahead with a hedge on the left, over the next stile and down to cross Mouse House Dike by a slab bridge. Cross the stile and go uphill with a fence on the right to reach a wooden fence at the top of the wood. Turn left for a yard or two to a stile into a field. Cross and head half left over the field, aiming well to the left of the buildings on the skyline, to a stile which soon becomes visible in the next fence. Cross this and keep forward up the next field to a stile in the wall on the left.

Turn right up the road (Clough Road), and opposite the farm (Kirkby Grange) at the top of the hill go down the lane on the left. A short distance before the buildings of Furnace Grange turn left down a concrete road for 50 yards and find a stile on the right in the hedge. (Here you join the Kirklees Way.) Cross the stile and the field to the next stile, then keep straight ahead, now with the hedge on the left. Halfway down the field, just after two large oak trees in the hedge, bear half right to a post at the bottom of the field. Cross a stone slab bridge and stile and turn left up the field with a hedge on the left. Cross the next stile and keep along the left hand edge of the next field to cross another stile and enter Leisure Lane (*the old name was Lazars Lane, a lazar being someone afflicted with leprosy, from Lazarus the beggar in St.Luke xvi.20. We know that in the Middle Ages there was a hospice for the poor and lepers run by monks in Emley*). Here you leave the Kirklees Way again.

Turn right up the lane. *If you look left you will see beyond the wall on the far side of the field the remains of former iron workings.* Walk straight through the yard of Thorncliffe Grange Farm (*notice the stately 17th-century farmhouse through a gateway on the left*), curve round to the right of a modern house and at the fork keep left along a hedged lane. At the next fork keep right past big modern houses to arrive at Church Street. Go left up the road past the church on the right and the Green Dragon on the left back to the start.

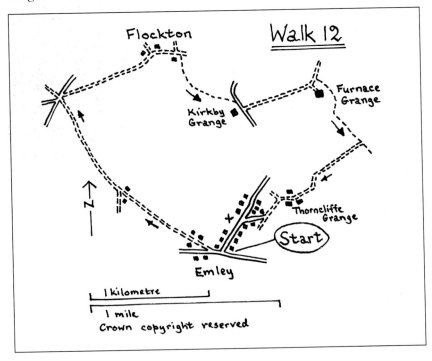

42

EMLEY TO BRETTON PARK

WALK 13

6¼ miles (10 km). Easy walking on field paths and old tracks, with an opportunity to visit the Yorkshire Sculpture Park.

By bus: **231/232 Huddersfield-Wakefield (half-hourly Mon-Sat, hourly Sun), 233 Huddersfield-Flockton (very infrequent, none on Sun), 934 link from Denby Dale Station (hourly, none on Sundays).**
By car: **Park in the car-park behind the post office which is beside the stump of the village cross in Emley village.**

From the car park at Emley Cross walk down Church Street to reach the Green Dragon. After passing the pub turn right along the first street (School Lane), follow it to its end and continue along a track (Tipping Lane), which soon narrows to a footpath to reach a road near a cottage. Turn right along the road for a few yards and then cross to go along a track behind cottages. When the track turns left at the end of the houses, keep forward along the left hand edge of the field with hedge/wall on the left to reach a stile in the field corner (*straight ahead can be seen the upper Dearne valley and the moors*).

Emley Church

Cross the stile and turn left with the hedge on the left to reach a stile in the next corner. Cross and keep on by the hedge/fence round a very large field. In the corner where the hedge makes its final bend to the right and heads down to Gillcar Farm, cross the stile by the gate on the left and walk forward over the field until you reach a cross track. Turn right down this to a concrete road and continue to join the main Wakefield-Denby Dale road. Cross the road and go down the lane opposite for about 160 yards to reach a stile on the left; cross the stile and the field to the far end. About 50 yards before you reach the far side of the field cross a stile on the left beside a large ash tree and turn right with the fence on the right to another stile by the side of the River Dearne. Cross this stile and head slightly left across a large field to a stile in the wall onto a road.

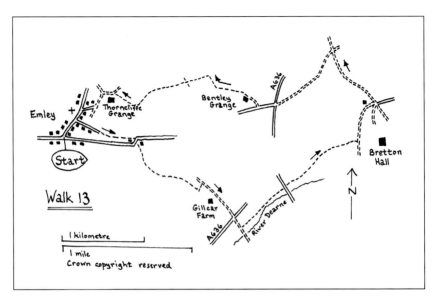

Cross the road and enter a small plantation (footpath sign), and follow the path through the trees to reach a stile by a gate into a field. Keep straight ahead with a fence on the left, and where the fence turns sharp left continue half left to reach a wooden bridge over Bentley Brook. Cross the bridge and go half left uphill to reach a stile on the skyline near trees; cross it and walk straight over the field to reach a fence. Carry on straight ahead with the fence on the left to reach Bretton Park. Turn left up the track. (*In a few yards a gap in the fence on the right or bearing right at the fork will give you access to the Yorkshire Sculpture Park*). The walk keeps left at the fork on a track which keeps the wood on the right. At the top of the hill the track bends right to a gate. Go through and keep forward along it.

Just before the access road to Bretton College go through a gate on the left and follow the track through Bretton Park (*fine views left over the Dearne valley*) to reach an iron gate. Pass through and keep forward. You are joined by a track from the right. In about 100 yards another track crosses yours. Here turn left downhill, eventually reaching the Wakefield-Denby Dale road again. Cross the road, turn left, and then right along the road to Emley. After 200 yards fork right along a track to Bentley Grange Farm.

Ignore the track forking left to the farmhouse and keep forward with a wall on the left and hedge on the right. Just before the entrance into the farmyard fork right through a gate and continue in the same direction with the farm buildings on the left. After leaving the farm the track follows a hedge on the left. Where the hedge changes from left to right; drop half right across the field to a stile in the corner. Cross the stile and a wooden bridge and bear left to a stile in the wall. Follow the path diagonally right uphill to stiles near the field corner (Emley mast is straight ahead). Cross the stile and head up with the fence on the left through one field; cross another stile and go slightly right uphill through a large field with trees (still aiming for the mast) to reach a stile in the hedge which is just to the right of one gate and 10 yards to the left of another. *In this area can be found the remains of bell pits dating from 1200 which were used to produce ironstone; this was taken to Foundry Grange to be smelted. The ironstone seam ran from Tankersley to Bradford.*

Cross the stile and follow the hedge/fence on the right to the stile by the gate in the next corner; cross it and immediately on the right climb stone steps in the wall into the next field; bear half left over the brow of the hill to reach a stile in the top left hand corner of the field beside a gateway (Thorncliffe Grange Farm indicates the direction). Cross the stile and follow the hedge on the left. Cross the stile in the top corner and turn left through the farmyard. Having passed to the right of a modern house keep left at the fork to cross a stile by a gate and continue along a hedged lane. At the next fork keep right past large modern houses. At Church Street turn left past the church and the Green Dragon to return to the start. *In the church boundary wall near the war memorial can be found the mediaeval Knights Hospitallers Cross of St John.*

The Cross of St John in the wall at Emley Church

AROUND EMLEY MOOR

WALK 14

7¼ miles (11½ km). Field paths and tracks in attractive undulating countryside, making a circuit of the television transmitter. Panoramic views. Drinks and snacks may be available at the Thorncliff Social Club, about two-thirds of the way round.

By bus: 231/232 Huddersfield-Wakefield (half-hourly Mon-Sat, hourly Sun), 233 Huddersfield-Flockton (very infrequent, none on Sun), 934 link from Denby Dale Station (hourly, none on Sundays).
By car: Park in the car-park behind the post office which is beside the stump of the village cross in Emley village.

Stand by the stump of the cross with your back to Church Street: facing you across the main road is a lane between buildings. Follow the lane to pass between Emley F.C.Supporters & Social Club and a car-park and continue along the fenced path. Where the wall on the left turns left, follow the path straight across the field towards some bungalows. Just before you reach them there is a small car park on the left and the recently created Emley Millennium Green on the right: do take time to stroll through this landscaped area to the roundel with the benches.

The path bears right along the nearside of the houses by a ginnel to a stile. Over it, turn left to another stile giving access to a farm-road. Cross a stile by a gate and descend the farm-road. Clayton West is straight ahead, Skelmanthorpe to the right. Where the track bears sharp right to Churchill Farm keep straight on to cross another stile to the **left** of a gate (ignoring the stile to the right of another gate!). A yard or two beyond this cross another stile and walk straight down the middle of the field to a stile by a gate in the hedge on the far side. Just beyond it is a second stile. Bear slightly left to the next stile in the hedge on the left immediately below the second gate. Cross it and walk down the hedge/wall on your right to another stile. Keep straight on to the next stile and a lane.

Turn left along it. Cross the stile by the first gate on the right and follow the wall on the left to a gate. Go through and bear slightly left down the large field to the next stile by a gate. A few yards ahead is another stile, then follow the hedge on your left. As you near the end of the field bear half right to drop and cross the beck by the bridge a few yards in front of a gate between two trees. Pass through the gate and continue with the wall on your left to a stile in the corner. Over it walk down the field for a few yards to a gate and a farm-road. Turn right along it.

At the motor road turn left downhill. Just before the bridge take the tarmac drive on the right, which soon becomes an unsurfaced walled lane. Pass through a narrow gap beside a gate. At the T-junction turn right past Baildon Place Farm; soon there is a left hand bend, but when the road bends right again to Silver Ings Farm keep straight on through a gate. Keep the hedge/fence on your right to a stile, then follow the right hand edge of the next field. When the fence on the right turns right, keep straight on, soon to pick up a hedge on the right. Follow this to a stile in a fence corner to the right of a gate ahead. Cross and with your back to the stile bear half right over towards the wood.

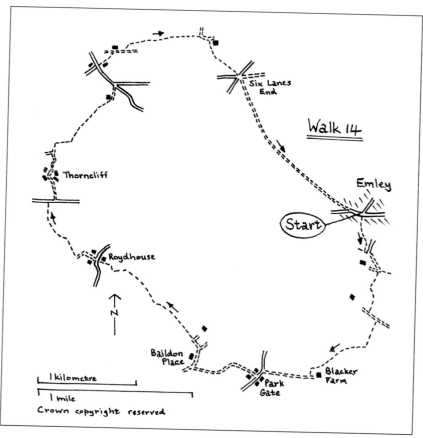

Six Lanes End

Walk 14

Thorncliff

Emley

Start

Roydhouse

N

Baildon Place

Park Gate

Blacker Farm

1 kilometre

1 mile

Follow the boundary-wall of the wood round to a stile. Cross it and the one just beyond it and turn right along the edge of the field and follow it all the way to a stile in the fence at the top. The next bit of the right of way is hard to follow, as the field boundaries have disappeared. Bear half left over the next enormous field, to the first solitary tree, then keep on in the same direction for about another 70 yards before turning left and heading for the next solitary tree (you may just about make out the old field boundary which you are following). There turn half right again up to a stile in the top corner of the field.

Cross the fenced track to a step-stile in the wall a few yards ahead. Over it follow the fence on your left to Roydhouse (there are pretty good views from here), cross the stile in the top corner of the field, another stile to the right of the gate ahead, and bear left to pass to the right of the barn and join the road over a stile. Turn right along the road for a few yards, then left along a lane before the Three Acres pub *(there's an Edward VII pillar box opposite the pub)*. Past the houses follow the walled lane through a gate and downhill (good views to Castle Hill, Huddersfield and the hills beyond).

Just before the gateway at the bottom turn sharp right over a stile and walk down the left hand edge of the field. Follow the hedge/fence/wall on your left over several stiles to the next road. Turn right for a few yards, then left up a farm-road. Cross the stile at the top and bear left along the track through Thorncliff. Pass between the houses (drinks and snacks may be available at the Social Club) and look carefully for a walled-lane going off on the right. Follow this. When you reach a fork keep right. After a few yards the lane ends at a field. Turn right along the wall on your right. Turn left along the next cross-wall, drop to a stile and cross the beck. Walk straight up the next large field, parallel to the wall on the left, and pass to the left of a solitary ash tree. About 150 yards after the tree bear left to the wall on your left and follow it up; where it bends left, keep forward across the field to the right hand end of Flockton Moor Top Farm.

In the course of 2002 this old farm will be rebuilt as a group of modern residences, so building works are likely to be in progress. An application has been made to divert the footpath and the likely new route is described here. Walk up the right hand boundary wall of the farm/new development. Bear left at the top and walk straight across the field to the road, probably aiming for a lamppost/road bends sign. Go left along the road, passing Long Lane on the right and Linfit Lane on the left *(another Edward VII pillar box here!)*; a few yards further on cross a gated stile on the right.

Keep forward over the field, passing a hedge corner, to another stile and then go half left up the next field to the next stile to the right of the cottages. Turn right along the road for 50 yards to a kissing-gate on the left. Go through, and with your back to the road bear half right across the field to a gate in the tall hedge. Continue with a fence on your right to cross two stiles, cross a farm-track, go through a kissing-gate and follow the wall on your left. Cross a stile and continue by the wall, which after a time is replaced by a hedge. At the T-junction turn right along a track towards the house, but immediately before it turn right down a walled-lane.

Follow this to the road at Six Lanes End. Cross straight over and walk up Crawshaw Lane opposite. Ignoring farm access roads keep left at the only fork and the lane will lead you back to Emley. When you reach the main road the car is a short distance to the left.

DENBY DALE, SKELMANTHORPE
AND BAGDEN PARK

WALK 15

4¾ miles (7½ km); tracks and field paths, with splendid views; there is one extremely steep climb.

By train: Denby Dale is on the Penistone Line, with trains from Huddersfield to Sheffield (roughly hourly Mon-Sat, two-hourly Sun).

By bus: 484 Leeds-Wakefield-Holmfirth (hourly, two-hourly on Sundays); 934 Denby Dale-Emley (village link) (hourly, no Sunday service); 236 Barnsley-Huddersfield (daily, two-hourly); 238 Huddersfield-Denby Dale (hourly; no Sunday service) to Denby Dale Interchange. Walkers arriving by train or bus should walk over to the start of the access road, then go through the gap in the fence on the left and follow the track downhill. At the foot continue forward to the main road. Turn left for 70 yards, then left again up Wesley Terrace.

By car: There is a free car park in the centre of Denby Dale opposite the post office and in front of the War Memorial. Park here. Turn right along the main road and in a few yards right again into Wesley Terrace.

Walk up Wesley Terrace and turn left after the Wesleyan Chapel (built 1799, enlarged 1859). Continue up the road for 100 yards and turn right along the track just before brick bungalow No.271. Go through a kissing-gate and follow the track to another gate. Turn right for a short distance, then left along the signposted path. On reaching Wither Wood (owned by the Woodland Trust and open to the public) turn right along the path between the wood and some bungalows. At the end turn left along the track. When the track drops, crosses an inconspicuous beck and begins to curve left, take a clear path leaving it on the right (in fact you walk straight on), which leads across three fields to a football pitch. Keep the same direction across the pitch to reach a street and turn right along it. You are now in Skelmanthorpe.

Turn right into a turning bay and pick up the path on the left behind the gardens. When it ends at a kissing-gate, keep on along the top edge of the field for a short way until the enclosed path begins again on the left. Follow it to a road. Now walk right for a yard or two to find a track on the right. Follow this to where it bears left, and in a few yards go right through a kissing-gate and walk down the field side to steps and a walled lane. Cross straight over and walk down through the wood to the main road (A636).

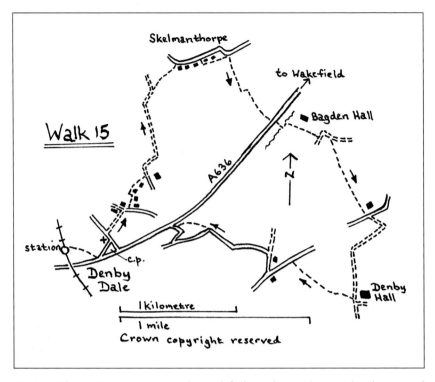

Skelmanthorpe

to Wakefield

Bagden Hall

Walk 15

A636

N

station

Denby
Dale

c.p.

Denby
Hall

1 kilometre

1 mile

Crown copyright reserved

Cross with caution to a gap-stile and follow the path straight down and across a footbridge over the River Dearne. Bear left up the other side and climb very steeply to a kissing-gate. Continue with the high wall of Bagden Hall on your left and then keep along with the iron railing to your left, ignoring all gates in it, until you reach another kissing-gate in the field corner. Turn left along the farm road (not sharp left back the way you have just come). In a few yards it turns right. After 100 yards fork right off the track up some steps to a kissing-gate, then walk half left over the field towards a fence corner. Go through the kissing-gate in this corner, then walk up with the fence posts on your left to some stone steps into Bagden Wood. Follow the clear path through the wood, crossing a track, and near the top edge of the wood bear right with the path to a stile out of the wood.

Bear slightly left up the next field, away from the hedge on the right, to find a footbridge over a ditch in the middle of the field, then keep the same line to a stile in the fence at the top. (This path has been officially diverted.) Keep the same line over the next field, i.e. bear slightly left from the stile, to a new stone stile in the wall ahead. Turn left along the

50

minor road for 30 yards, then right up a track. From the brow of the hill there are extensive views over Deffer Wood to Barnsley. Follow the track to Denby Hall Farm. A short distance after the first buildings on the right, and opposite an entrance into the farm on the left, cross a stile by a large gate on the right and walk straight forward to join a track which leads to another stile by a gate in the far right hand corner.

Now bear half-right to a solitary tree in the middle of the field; from it look slightly left and you will see a step-stile in the wall ahead. Cross it and follow the wall on your left to a stile in it near the far corner. Turn left along the road to the junction (Exley Gate) where you turn right. Bear left with the main road at the next junction. Just past the entrance into Pingle Nook on the right, fork right off the road down a track which becomes an old lane. Follow this down and cross the footbridge over the Dearne. Go left for thirty yards, then turn right up a road which leads back to the main road.

Turn left to return to the centre of Denby Dale, *passing the Pie Hall, where flowers are planted in the tin in which in 1964 the record 6½ ton meat pie was baked. Proceeds from the sale of this pie paid for the Village Hall behind.* To return to the Interchange, fork right at the Dalesman pub.

Footbridge over the River Dearne

DENBY DALE TO BIRK HOUSE AND UPPER CUMBERWORTH

WALK 16

5 miles (8 km). Lovely countryside, woodland and parkland, field paths and old tracks, some fine houses and splendid views.

By train: Denby Dale is on the Penistone Line, with trains from Huddersfield to Sheffield (roughly hourly Mon-Sat, two-hourly Sun).

By bus: 484 Leeds-Wakefield-Holmfirth (hourly, two-hourly on Sundays); 934 Denby Dale-Emley (village link) (hourly, no Sunday service); 236 Barnsley-Huddersfield (daily, two-hourly); 238 Huddersfield-Denby Dale (hourly; no Sunday service) to Denby Dale Interchange. Walkers arriving by train or bus should walk over to the start of the access road, then go through the gap in the fence on the left and follow the track downhill. At the foot continue forward to the main road. Cross it and turn left, then right down Norman Road.

By car: There is a free car park in the centre of Denby Dale opposite the post office and in front of the War Memorial. Park here. Cross the main road and turn right, then left down Norman Road.

Walk down Norman Road, cross the road at the bottom and continue up Trinity Drive. Pass the church and take the left hand of three paths across the field, the unsurfaced one over the grass. Cross a stile beside the gate into the wood and follow the path through the wood until steps lead up to a road. Turn left along it. Ignore the first large gateway on the opposite side of the road, but immediately after the second (entrance to Inkerman House) cross the road and walk up a walled lane. Pass through a tunnel under the railway and follow the ascending path. When you reach the top of the wood on the right, ignore the path straight ahead across the field towards the houses and turn right to continue by the wall on your right (with the wood beyond) to a metal kissing-gate, then keep on along the walled lane to a junction.

Turn right, but immediately fork left along another walled lane. After a time the track leads round outside the wood. A few yards before the end of the wood, with a gate and stile straight ahead, fork right on a narrow path close to the left hand edge of the field. Cross a stile just before a gate, and after passing along the edge of a field now with the wall on your right you are soon back in a walled lane. At the end of this cross the stile to the right of the gate and follow the wall on your right down to cross a beck and climb the other side to a stile. Turn right along the track. Ignore a walled lane coming in from the left and pass a farm entrance on the right, and where the track drops and curves right turn left through a swing-gate by a larger gate into the trees.

Walk straight through this parkland, keeping a short way from the wall to your left. Where this wall comes closer, and about 50 yards before a gate ahead, leave the path and drop half-right through the trees to a stile in the wall. Keep the same direction across the field towards the next wood, to find a stile in the wall. Drop steeply down to cross a footbridge over the River Dearne. Cross the stile and turn left along the fenced path, ignoring the stile in the fence ahead. Opposite the next stile on the right cross a stile on the left and immediately cross a beck by a stone slab to enter Upper Dearne Woodland.

Walk forward for a short distance, then bear right on a path through the rhododendrons, soon bearing right again at a marker post along a path which for a few yards is gravelled. The path leads to a footbridge. Cross the track by stiles and continue forward on the path through the wood.

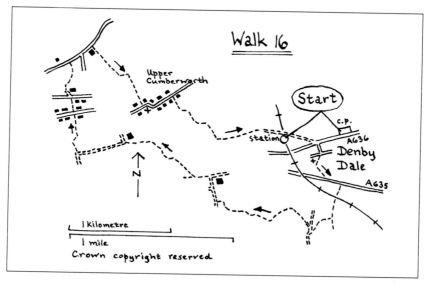

Now you are walking parallel to the beck down on the left. When the way seems to be barred by a wall (where a ginnel comes in from the right), bear left down towards the beck and then continue in the same direction as before. As you approach the far end of the wood, keep right at a fork to reach a step-stile out of the wood. Keep forward with the fence on your right to the next stile.

Turn left along the track. Where it turns sharp left, follow the footpath sign right and walk down with the wall on your left. Cross the beck and bear right to the edge of the field. Now turn left and walk up with the wall on your right, passing through a stile, to another stile onto the road. Cross diagonally left to a stile in the wall opposite. Walk straight down to the main road (fine views ahead). Cross the road and walk a few yards right to take a farm access road on the left. After about 20 yards fork slightly left off it and walk down to an old stone gatepost, then keep down to pass to the left of a house and a recently planted avenue of trees, curving right with it to reach a stile in the wall on the left. Walk straight over the next field, passing to the left of a telegraph pole, to another stile. Cross the beck and walk straight over the field to a stile onto the road.

Turn right. Pass the end of Heater Lane on the right and continue along Birkhouse Lane. At the end of the buildings of Birk House Farm on the right turn right along a track. Where this ends at a stile by a gate bear slightly left across the next field to cross a beck and a stile at a line of trees. Keep in the same direction towards a large group of farm buildings in the distance. When you meet a cross-wall turn left along it. At a wide fenced gap in this wall there is a stile. Cross it and walk straight up the middle of the next field, aiming to the right of the farm. Cross another stile and keep on up with the wall on your left to another stile and the road.

Turn left through Upper Cumberworth. As you near the end of the houses, there are redbrick bungalows on the right. Follow the footpath sign along a ginnel between two of these to a stile into a field. Keep forward, picking up a hedge on your left, but at a stile in it cross into the next field and bear half right over the field to a stile in a wall corner. Cross it and follow the wall on the right and stay with it when it turns right, to reach another stile in the next corner. Cross the road and stile opposite and then walk slightly left to the far corner of the field. There cross the stile into a fenced path round what used to be the edge of the quarry. This ends at a stile.

Now turn left along with the fence on your left. Follow this for quite some distance, until it becomes a high metal mesh fence, at which point you will see a large gate ahead. A stile beside it takes you into a fenced track which brings you down to a concrete road. Here keep straight on, over the railway, to Denby Dale Interchange. Car drivers should now follow the directions given to those arriving by bus, to return to the car-park.

DENBY DALE TO GUNTHWAITE
AND BIRDS EDGE

WALK 17

6½ miles (10½ km). Field paths and old tracks through undulating countryside, with woodland and streams, extensive views and several fine old buildings, including Gunthwaite Hall and Tithe Barn and Bird's Edge Friends' Meeting House.

By train: Denby Dale is on the Penistone Line, with trains from Huddersfield to Sheffield (roughly hourly Mon-Sat, two-hourly Sun).

By bus: 484 Leeds-Wakefield-Holmfirth (hourly, two-hourly on Sundays); 934 Denby Dale-Emley (village link) (hourly, no Sunday service); 236 Barnsley-Huddersfield (daily, two-hourly); 238 Huddersfield-Denby Dale (hourly; no Sunday service) to Denby Dale Interchange. Walkers arriving by train or bus should walk down the access road to the main road and turn right under the viaduct.

By car: There is a free car park in the centre of Denby Dale opposite the post office and in front of the War Memorial. Park here. Turn right along the main road to the viaduct and pass under it.

Gunthwaite Tithe Barn

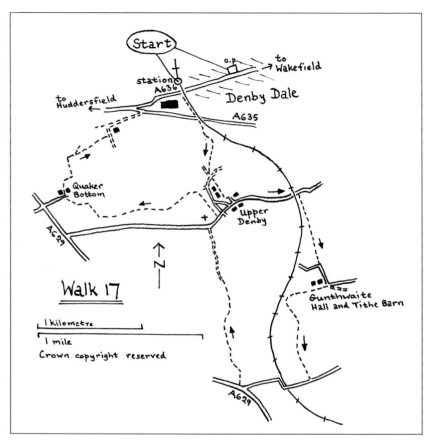

Immediately after passing under the railway viaduct cross the main road and go down the steps, to take the path along the mill fence, keeping the viaduct on your left. Cross the Barnsley Road (A635) and take the signposted bridleway opposite. Just past the houses ignore a large gate on the right into Hagg Wood and continue along the bridleway, which soon becomes cobbled and follows the left hand edge of the wood. At the top of the hill there is a bench with a fine view of the Dearne valley. Continue up the walled path to a junction.

Between the track on the left and the track straight ahead there is a squeeze stile. Go through and walk up the field side, pass through another stile and walk between gardens. Cross a tarmac drive and keep forward along the walled track. On reaching a street, keep forward along it past a row of garages. Take the first street on the right (Fairfields) and

56

Gunthwaite Hall

turn left at the T-junction (Lower Denby Lane). On the right is the George pub. Here we join for a short distance the Barnsley Boundary Walk. Immediately after the railway bridge cross the road and mount the stone steps (from here you have a distant view of Barnsley). Walk along the fenced path on the top edge of the field, cross a stile and descend into a wood.

Keep along the foot of the railway embankment and cross a stile into a field. Walk along the right hand edge of the field for 30 yards to a redundant stile, then bear half left across the field towards a solitary tree. Keep the same line over the middle of the field to follow a row of telegraph poles to the far side. Keep forward along the track, pass through the gap in the field corner, follow the track to the next road and continue along it. When the road turns sharp left, go through the gateway on the right. Gunthwaite Tithe Barn, timber-framed on a stone base, is to the right, and a little further on parts of the former Gunthwaite Hall (17th-century) can also be seen on the right. Continue along the track.

At a fork, where the right hand branch leads to a tunnel under the railway, keep left. Soon the track bears left, with the high railway embankment on the right, then drops through a wood. Leave the wood through a bridle-gate and follow the track along the left hand edge of several fields to the next road and turn right. Turn right along the A629 for 50 yards, then right again through the second gate. Follow the wall on the right round two sides of the field and go through the waymarked gate in the far corner. Pass through several more gates, and having passed through one on the right, turn left and walk down, now with the wall on your left. Cross the beck and continue up the enclosed path, cross another beck and follow the walled lane up to Upper Denby, where you reach the main road near the church.

Cross the road and turn right, enter Upper House Fold, walk to the wall at the back and take the footpath on the left. Follow the wall on the right with the cricket field to your left. Go through a gate followed by two stiles then a gateway, then keep forward to cross a stile in the hedge/wall and turn left up the track. At the end ignore the gate ahead, cross the stile on the left and follow the wall on your right. Continue over seven more stiles (ignoring a stile in the wall on the right between numbers four and five), turn left for a few yards along a track and cross a stile on the right. Follow the wall on the right to the next stile by a

lamppost. Turn right, go through the gate into Moor Royd and pass to the left of the house to a stile into a field.

Follow the wall on the left down. Shortly before the wooden chalet cross the stile on the left and walk along the bottom edge of the next field. Cross a stile on the way, then another stile by the gate, go half right over the tarmac drive to a stile on the right of a large tree, and follow the wall on the left down a paved path to a small gate. A steep flight of steps leads down to the valley bottom. Go through a metal gate and ascend with a wall on the right. More steps lead to a metal kissing-gate.

"A steep flight of steps..."

58

Turn right down the cobbled lane between the attractive houses of Quaker Bottom. Keep left at the fork to find on the left the Friends' Meeting House. Walk along the track and cross the stile by the gate ahead.

Quaker Bottom

Follow the track as it bears right downhill. Immediately before a gateway ahead, beside a large holly tree, turn left and walk along to the left of a row of holly trees, but 30 yards before the end of the field slip right through the old wall and continue in the same direction as before. Where the wall on the left bends left, fork right, down to a stile in another wall corner. Walk straight down the field with the railway viaduct in the distance and a fine view left to Emley Moor and Upper Cumberworth. Head for a walled lane on the far side of the field and follow it to a T-junction where you turn left. The lane curves right past a large converted farmhouse and drops to the A635. Cross the road, turn left, then soon hard right at the next junction to return to Denby Dale.